# Luis Suárez

## To the Top!

2012: Competes in the London Olympic Games for Uruguay.

2011: The Liverpool club reaches an agreement with Ajax for the acquisition of Suarez for 27 million euros in January.

Uruguay is crowned champion at the 2011 Copa America. Luis named Player of the Tournament.

After a match against Manchester United on October 15, Luis is accused of uttering racist slurs against player Patrice Evra.

2010: Luis Suarez summoned to the Uruguay national team to play the FIFA World Cup in South Africa, in June. On July 2, saves a goal with his hand and becomes an international villain but a hero in Uruguay.

2009: Marries Sofia Balbi, his childhood girlfriend, in March.

2007: Signs a five-year contract with Ajax for 7.5 million euros.

Debuts with the Uruguayan National team in a match against Colombia in February.

2006: Netherlands team Groningen signs Luis Suarez for 800,000 euros. Luis moves to Europe.

2005: Begins his professional career in soccer with the National Football Club at age 14.

Makes his debut at the National Junior Team against Ottawa, in the Copa Libertadores, in May.

Scores his first goal for Libertadores on September 10.

1994: Moves with his family to Montevideo, the Uruguayan capital.

1987: Born in Salto, Uruguay, on January 24.

## Personal File

**Name:** Luis Alberto Suárez Díaz

**Nicknames:** Gunner, Bunny, Predator

**Place of Birth:** Salto, Uruguay

**Nationality:** Uruguayan

**Zodiac Sign:** Aquarius

**Height:** 5 foot 11 (1.81 m)

**Twitter:** @luis16suarez

**Position:** Forward

**Number for Liverpool:** 7

**Exploits:** A goal every 135 minutes during his season with Ajax.

149 goals in 264 official matches since his career's start.

ISBN-13: 978-1-4222-2656-8 (hc) — 978-1-4222-9197-9 (ebook)

Printing (last digit) 9 8 7 6 5 4 3 2 1
Printed and bound in the United States of America.
CPSIA Compliance Information: Batch #S2013. For further
information, contact Mason Crest at 1-866-MCP-Book.

**ABOUT THE AUTHORS:**
Gustavo Vazquez-Lozano was born in Aguascalientes, Mexico. He is a writer and independent publisher. He is the author of *La estrella del sur* (Ediciones SM, 2003) and *Everything About the Beatles* (Otras Inquisiciones, 2010).

Federico Vargas Benard was born in Mexico City. He is regular contributor to the sports section in *La Jornada de Aguascalientes* newspaper.

**Photo credits:** EFE / Jon Hrusa: 4; EFE / Lavandeira Jr : 14; Getty Images: 22; Library of Congress: 30; Liverpool F.C.: 24; © 2012 Photos.com, a division of Getty Images: 11; DSPA / Shutterstock.com: 17; Katatonia82 / Shutterstock.com: 20; Herbert Kratky / Shutterstock.com: 26; Wikimedia: 1, 2, 10, 16, 19, 25.

# TABLE OF CONTENTS

CHAPTER 1. The Hand of God                          5

CHAPTER 2. The European Adventure                   9

CHAPTER 3. South Africa 2010                        15

CHAPTER 4. Light and Darkness                       21

CHAPTER 5. The Uruguayan Hope                       27

FURTHER READING                                     30

INTERNET RESOURCES                                  31

INDEX                                               32

Luis Suarez (right) stops the ball with his hand in the goal line during the 2010 World Cup, in a quarterfinals match between Urugay and Ghana, on July 2, 2010.

# The Hand of God

HOW MUCH AGONY AND EUPHORIA CAN BE COMPRESSED INTO in one minute of play? The answer can be found in the clash between Uruguay and Ghana during the FIFA World Cup tournament played in South Africa on July 2, 2010. The way that game ended was, for many, the most dramatic moment of the entire tournament.

## "There is a God and He is Uruguayan"

What was at stake between Ghana and Uruguay was no small thing. The winner would advance to the World Cup semi-finals and be considered one of the world's top four teams. It was the 120th minute of the game—90 minutes of regulation game plus 30 overtime—but the furious match continued tied at 1-1. Neither team was willing to renounce the dream of lifting the trophy. In the last minute of the match, the Africans made a powerful center pass that over-matched the Uruguayan goalkeeper. Desperate, Uruguay's star forward Luis Suarez ran to the goal line in an effort to prevent the tragedy. On Ghana's first shot, the ball hit his leg. There would be another shot, a direct header right at the net, that the crowd believed would be the end of Uruguay's dream of World Cup victory. The Uruguayan goalkeeper was beaten. Only Luis Suarez was in front of the goal.

Then Suarez did the unthinkable, an action that the world would unanimously criticize—especially Africa—but one that would win him acclaim throughout Uruguay, as if he were a modern Robin Hood. Suarez prevented the goal, using his hand!

The referee's reaction was as expected: he granted Ghana a penalty shot and expelled Suarez from the field. The player walked away covered in tears before the television cameras. But the Sky Blue team and millions of Uruguayans who were watching the game on TV with long faces, didn't suspect that Ghana would fail to convert the penalty shot. Now the tears were on Dominic Adiyiah's face, the African forward, and the joy was on Luis's side, the enfant terrible of soccer, who was jumping euphorically on the bench. His sacrifice had been worth it.

## Hero or Villain?

Surely no other action in the field could divide public opinion more about a player. Only a great soccer star could be at the center of such a storm and come out clean. Luis Suarez is used to controversy, as well as to making spectacular plays.

The criticism that Suarez received after the game with Ghana showed that to many people he was a villain. Ghana's coach called him a cheater, while a Cape Town newspaper declared, "Africa was robbed." The news was flooded by reproaches for his action.

In Uruguay, though, Luis was regarded as a hero. In fact, in this soccer-loving nation of 3.5 million people, you would be hard-pressed to find a soul that did not believe Luis had accomplished a great thing that day. His teammate Diego Forlan spoke for all his colleagues when he said, "Suarez is a hero. He didn't score a goal, but he saved one and now we are in the semifinal."

The dramatic episode with Ghana is a good sample of everything that Luis Suarez is known for: passionate, committed, fiery play, as well as controversial behavior. Some say he was a "holy terror" during his teen years growing up in Montevideo. The contrary was true however. Luis was a normal child who, like so many other soccer super stars, learned to play in the best school ever: the streets.

## Playing in the Streets

This story begins in a poor neighborhood of El Salto, Uruguay. It was there that Luis Alberto Suarez Diaz was born on January 24, 1987. Salto is Uruguay's second biggest city. His father's name was Rodolfo and played soccer as well. His mother was Sandra. His parents were simple workers with seven children to provide for. The economic situation was difficult and the family made a lot of sacrifices. He lived with his family near the military camps. "The house was like a hundred yards from the barracks' court, and this was the kids' meeting place," recalls older brother Paolo, who invited him to play with his friends at an early age.

Luis and Paolo found their greatest joy in soccer. They spent all day playing in the street. Luis played so well that the coaches thought he was older. At four years old he ran faster with the ball than without it. "Our routine was to get up early and spend all day outside with the ball. We went home to eat when there was food at home, and there wasn't always," says Paolo.

## To Montevideo

In 1994 the Suarez family took their belongings and moved south to Montevideo in search for a better life. Once there Luis began to study at the primary school. As they settled, his parents started looking for a club where Luis could play. His parents took him to the Urreta, a team where other top players, such as Diego Lugano, had been raised. At six years old Luis began scoring for the club.

In stark contrast to this early happiness, the seven children of the Suarez family endured the trauma of their parents' separation. The mother then had to make greater sacrifices to make ends meet. When Luis was twelve he was already attracting the attention of Uruguayan soccer teams. He daydreamed of becoming a

**Fast Fact**

Both Luis's father and grandfather played for the National Football Club. Luis's father, Rodolfo Suarez, also played as a right fielder at Salto.

great striker. His idol was Gabriel Batistuta, the Argentinean legend. At eleven he was invited to attend a youth camp in La Plata, Argentina, but he had to decline the offer because he could not afford the boots required.

Trying to forget the sadness of his parents' separation, Conejito ("Bunny"), as his friends called him, was going to dances and spending long hours at his friends' homes, so much that his mother and brother Paolo rebuked him. "I knew that he was a great player and I was mad to see him waste his talent," Paolo recalls.

## In the ranks of National

Luis began his long climb in the youth forces of the National Football Club. The club was founded in the late nineteenth century and considered one of the best

A difficult moment in the life of Luis and his siblings Diego, Maxi, Leticia, Giovana, and Paolo came when their parents separated. Soccer became a kind of consolation in the midst of a dire financial situation. The streets—where so many soccer legends have sprung up—was where Luis and Paolo learned and developed their skills.

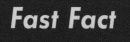

## Fast Fact

Luis's older brother Paolo gained Salvadoran citizenship in order to play with the Selecta, El Salvador's national soccer team.

clubs in South America. In over one hundred years, National has won the championship 43 times in Uruguay.

At 14 years old he was entering the formative forces of the Tricolores (three-colored team), in which he made rapid progress thanks to his natural talent. His days were full of soccer and studying at night for of which his favorite subject was math. Although he was still just a boy his talent propelled him to play in third, fourth and fifth divisions. Luis was able to score goals in all of them.

## An ultimatum

From these years comes one of the most memorable legends about Luis Suarez, who is also nicknamed "the Gunner." Unfortunately he was drawn by the siren songs of dancing and nightlife and was not

mature enough to set limits.

The legend says that one day he was called by his coach Ricardo Perdomo to a hazy dressing room; the coach began shaking him and yelled bitterly, "You start to train and focus your life, or get out of here!" From that moment, Luis realized that if he wanted to do something with his life, to be part of the lineup of the National soccer team, he would have to change. He realized it was not enough to just be good with the ball.

Was this legend truth or lie? Whatever the answer, the truth in this story represents a moment in Suarez's life: the talented teenager in danger of losing the way, ignoring the promise, and one day the commitment to the team. Furthermore in his own words he said, "There were many problems . . . but I realized that soccer was my thing and if I didn't give myself that chance at 14, I was not going to do it anymore." The reward came quickly and like all good things came at the right time. At 16 he was part of main team and two years later he finally debuted with National in the Copa Libertadores. The dream had begun.

# The European Adventure

SUAREZ HAD TURNED DOWN OFFERS FROM OTHER TEAMS in order to sign with National. On March 3, 2005, his dedication paid off when he was called to debut professionally in the Copa Libertadores. Thereafter, he began to realize his full potential. He scored his first goal at the professional level on September 10, 2005.

## Champion with the Tricolores

Since his first year with El Bolso (the National club team), Luis stood out and began to attract the attention of European clubs. During the 2005-2006 seasons with the Tricolores he had great performances. He contributed 12 goals in 34 games, helping his team to lift the League Trophy that same year. At age 18, Suarez had achieved things that most people can only dream of: he debuted in Copa Libertadores, gained membership in the main team, and was a champion with National.

## Sofia

Soccer was not his only love. As a boy in Montevideo, Luis had met a girl who would become the most important woman in his life. Her name was Sofia Balbi. They got engaged when she was just 12 and Luis was 15, but their story

**Facade of Grand Central Park Stadium, home of the National Football Club.**

was destined to endure. Luis spent much time at her house. Sofia's support was very important for him; she exerted a positive influence on the young man who had so much pain inside. The love affair would have to suffer the ordeal of separation again. Just a few months later, Sofia arrived with the news that his parents were moving to Spain and they would not see each other again. "When I came to Barcelona," says Sofia, "the day before I'll never forget. We went for a walk and sat at a bus stop and we both started to cry, and did not stop

because we believed that we were not going to see each other again."

Although Luis had lost her for the moment he had a very clear objective in mind: to play, to move forward in the ranks of National, going as far as Europe, near his girlfriend. The illusion of being with her gave him greater impetus to keep on studying and practicing soccer. When Sofia went to Europe, the couple kept in contact by letter and promised to meet again someday. Neither suspected that the opportunity was closer than they thought.

## A Visit from the Netherlands

One day some scouts from Groningen in the Netherlands arrived in Montevideo to see Elias Figueroa play. Elias was then a player of the Liverpool Football Club of Montevideo. They were contemplating his possible recruitment. Over the weekend, the visitors also saw Luis Suarez. Luis would later say it was "the best game I had in Uruguay," and the scouts decided to take him instead. It was written in the stars that the Bunny would be the one to pack his bags for the Netherlands.

His real international career began at 19. It was a contract for 800,000 euros—a bargain considering what he would do for the team in that season. "When the call came from Europe I didn't think twice," he would later admit. "The first thing that came to mind was being near Sofia."

## In the Netherlands

Groningen is a fancy student town north of the Netherlands. Luis's great European adventure would begin here. From the outset, things were not easy. First, there was little culturally or geographically that linked the Netherlands with Uruguay. Besides the distance, there was the language barrier and the need to adapt to life in northern Europe. At first, these difficulties brought the Bunny's playing level down, and he was even relegated to the second division team. Regardless of the difficult transition giving up was not an option. Hard work and discipline produced his famous displays of talent in the field, and they revived his hope and also his team's. "I was always clear that I was not going to give up and would soon have the opportunity to prove my worth," he said.

## The Much-Expected Date

His determination to learn Dutch won him the esteem of his peers. Bruno Silva, another Uruguayan who had played in Groningen, was a key support in the adjustment. Meanwhile, another long-awaited meeting took place in Spain. After a year of correspondence, Luis had finally reunited with Sofia. He also asked her for help.

"I was still a child. I didn't speak English or Dutch. When I signed the contract, I had twelve days off and went to Barcelona, because Sofia was there, and

**View of the historic harbor in the Dutch city of Groningen, where Luis played in 2006-07.**

said to her 'Come with me.' Her father gave her permission to show me around, since she spoke English."

Suarez made his debut for Groningen in the "miracle match," as he calls it. They were playing against Partisan, and he was called as a replacement ten minutes before the end. These minutes were enough for the striker to score twice and create a penalty. Since then, Luis continued to help the club win more victories. In his year with Groningen he scored 11 goals in 33 matches, teamed with forward Erik Nevland, and, with his impeccable technique, sparked interest from other clubs.

Despite the disciplinary problems—yellow and red cards—after a year with the team Luis was already a well-regarded figure and his transfer to a more powerful squad seemed imminent. It was then that a truly legendary team in the Netherlands and Europe requested his services.

## Ajax the Great

The next European stop was the powerful team Ajax, so named for the warrior of Greek mythology. Ajax was one of the three clubs that dominate the Dutch league and according to sports historians, the seventh most successful European club of the twentieth century. There were some surprises in the transfer to the new team. First, Groningen rejected an initial offer of 3.5 million euros. Ajax raised the offer to 7.5 million. The deal was finalized when Luis threatened to take his case to arbitration if Groningen blocked the transfer.

Eventually Suarez became an idol in that city and took a giant step in his career. His market value had increased and a new world of possibilities was opened. "When I look back and think of all the friends in the neighborhood," he reflected upon learning the news, "in those half-ruined, dusty soccer fields on the streets of Montevideo which I traveled with the ball, I feel very proud."

Luis played 44 games and scored 22 goals in his first year with Ajax. In no time, he was proving to the club why the purchase had been a good decision.

## Ajax Captain

The 2009-2010 seasons began with a very special honor for the Gunner. New coach Martin Jol, impressed within the first two weeks, decided to name him the team's captain. As captain of Ajax, the Uruguayan scored 35 goals in 33 games, ranking as top scorer not only on the team, but through-

Luis Suarez debuted with Uruguay's national team on February 8, 2007, in a match against Colombia, which the Blue Sky won by a score of 3-1. However, the happy occasion was marred because Luis was expelled after receiving two yellow cards.

out the European continent in terms of goals per game.

Suarez was the new and undisputed star in the Netherlands. At the end of that season, he won the award for best player in the Dutch league. IFFHS also named him Top Scorer in the world, and Luis claimed the Golden Boot trophy in the local competition.

## Two Finals, Four Goals

In that same year Ajax was in the Dutch Cup final, or KNVB Cup, a knockout competition that gets a lot of attention. In 2010 the championship was decided between the two biggest rivals of Dutch soccer, Ajax and arch-rival Feyenoord. The match raised a lot of controversy and it had to be divided in two matches, one in Amsterdam and the other in the De Kuip stadium in Rotterdam. This arrangement had not been made since 1983. Safety was a priority for the authorities considering the strong rivalry between the clubs.

The first match at the Amsterdam Arena was of irrefutable quality. Captain Luis Suarez and his players crushed a strong Feyenoord squad, beating them 2-0. The next match, played on May 6, would be one of Luis Suarez's finest hours. Within just four minutes into the game, Suarez recovered the ball in the midfield and dribbled fast to the edge of the goal area. He drew an impressive cross shot and defeated the goalkeeper. This early goal, in a hostile stadium and crowd, was indispensable for Ajax. When the game was about to end,

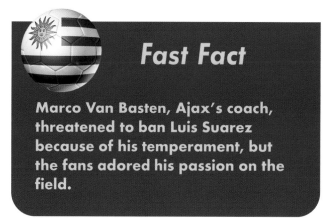

**Fast Fact**

Marco Van Basten, Ajax's coach, threatened to ban Luis Suarez because of his temperament, but the fans adored his passion on the field.

Suarez put the last nail in the local team's coffin: after a showdown with the Feyenoord goalkeeper inside the goal area, he placed a cross shot to put the fourth and winning goal on the scoreboard. It was undoubtedly one of the brightest moments of his ascending career.

**Fast Fact**

Uruguayan Bruno Silva was playing for Groningen when Luis Suarez came to the Netherlands. He helped Luis adapt to the new environment. They have become great friends since then.

Luis celebrates his first goal during the match against Mexico in the group stage of the 2010 World Cup, at the Royal Bafokeng stadium in South Africa, June 22, 2010.

# South Africa 2010

SOCCER IS URUGUAY'S MOST POPULAR SPORT, AND RIGHTLY SO. The first World Cup was held in Montevideo in 1930, as part of the celebration of a century of independence. The "Charruas"—as Uruguayan players are called—have been crowned world champions twice. Nobody has won the Copa America more times than Uruguay.

Every four years, the nearness of a World Cup awakens excitement, dreams, and the hope of being world champions once again. Until summer 2010, the recent history of the Blue Sky team had not given many reasons for celebration. With the exception of the 2002 World Cup held in Korea-Japan, they had been outside the tournament for the last twenty years. However, with a new generation of international stars such as Diego Forlan, Sebastian Abreu, Maxi Pereira, and Luis Suarez, the hopes of the nation were rising. There was a feeling of anticipation in the air throughout the country.

## A Difficult Start

After his brilliant performance in the Netherlands, Luis Suarez had his place secured in the Uruguayan team that would go to South Africa. They were lead by coach Washington Tabarez. Diego Forlan, Edinson Cavani, and Luis made a very effective scoring triad. These three men would give the world a

**Washington "The Master" Tabarez is considered one of the best strategists in modern times and is widely respected inside the soccer fraternity.**

lot to talk about in the coming month of competition.

Uruguay's arrival to the World Cup had not been easy. Tabarez's team had finished fifth in the qualifying round and had to play off against Costa Rica. During qualifying, Luis had a hard time. Criticism rained down from the press that unfairly compared him with the team's most visible representative, Diego Forlan. Despite these attacks and an initial poor performance, both Suarez and Tabarez held on and were

able to put the team in the World Cup.

To some extent, the group stage favored the squad. As part of Group A, Uruguay would face two rivals with not much international credibility, Mexico and host South Africa. However, the fourth team in the group was France, which was ranked second-best in the world. The Uruguayans hoped to make a good showing. They never imagined that life was going to smile at them like never before.

## "I'm Sky Blue"

The World Cup did not begin in the best way for Luis. Uruguay played against France in its first game of the group stage, and tension was high. The match was a goalless draw; not the best outcome for either of the two teams. However, the Charruas were only beginning one of the sweetest stories in Uruguayan soccer history.

During the second match, the team left its insecurities back in the hotel and confronted the host South Africa. It was a life or death situation for Tabarez's students. When the game ended, it was Diego Forlan, not Luis, who was carried on the shoulders but even when Forlan was the star of the game, Luis was a key player. He drew the penalty that led to the second goal

Although the country of Uruguay has fewer than 4 million people, it has one of the most successful national soccer teams in the world. The Sky Blue has been crowned champions in 20 FIFA competitions, including two World Cups, two Olympic Games, 15 Copa Americas, and a Gold Cup.

and recorded the assist for Uruguay's third and final goal of the game.

The last match of the group stage, against Mexico, was perfect for Suarez. He started nervously, but there was something different. He tried the left side of the field, the right side; he played for the team and went alone when necessary. In the 43rd minute he got his reward. A perfect center pass by Cavani left him with a clear goal opportunity. The striker made no mistake, and Uruguay had won its place in the World Cup quarterfinals.

## Quarterfinals

The World Cup's next phase sent them against South Korea. An early goal by Luis gave the Charruas an advantage, but the team seemed distracted. The Asian team took advantage of that and scored in the 68th minute to tie things up. With time running out, Uruguay was attacking with everything. Korea was resisting as well as it could. That is when Luis' genius appeared once more. He took the ball inside the goal area, made a cut toward the center, and made a curling shot to the second goalpost with the inside of his right foot. It seemed like an impossible trajectory, but he scored one of the most beautiful goals of the tournament.

"I could not believe it," he said after the game. "I did not realize that the ball was going to enter. All I want now is to enjoy." For Suarez, everything seemed to be according to a wonderful previously written script: there were goals, assists, and unani-

**Luis was expected to help superstar Diego Forlan lead La Celeste in the World Cup.**

mous recognition to his skill. It was the perfect World Cup. However, like everything in this player's life, controversy and drama also demanded a place.

## A Nation in Suspense

Meanwhile, in Uruguay World Cup fever had taken hold of the national life. Everyone remembered the Sky Blue team's past glories and the stars seemed to be aligning favorably. The government itself supported the "Futbol Friday" celebrations. "On Fridays, employees of private

**Fast Fact**

Luis married Sofia, his childhood sweetheart, in Amsterdam and Montevideo. The honeymoon was in the Bora-Bora islands of French Polynesia.

and public companies could go to work in the shirt of the Uruguayan National Selection," writes journalist Alejandro Figueredo. "The streets were full of flags, the cars were decorated with patriotic accessories and all that was talked about was soccer."

The team's chef had packed everything for South African lands, including a sweet treat for the boys before the quarterfinals; food that the players would want but would be impossible to find on the continent: quince candy, sweet potato, milk candy, and 180 kilos of tea. Finally, on July 2 Ghana clashed against Uruguay for a place in the semifinal. The whole country was expecting an easy, dispassionate game, and already dreaming of the next phase.

## The Best Match in South Africa

The game against Ghana seemed ideal for Uruguay to win without problems. Ghana was not a highly regarded team. But Africa's last survivors in the tournament had other plans. They were ready to qualify or die trying. The regulation game ended with a 1-1 tie and went into overtime.

It was, for many, the best match of the 2010 World Cup, at least where drama and action are concerned. In the last minute of the second overtime, with the score still tied, it seemed that the teams would have to go to a tiebreaker with penalty kicks. Before that, Ghana mounted its last attack. After several headers, the ball was in the air and the goal unguarded. Luis, desperate to avoid the collapse of Uruguay's hopes, stopped the ball with his hand. He was expelled, but that action allowed the Sky Blue team by a cruel twist of fate for the Africans to reach the semifinals. Africa, some said, had been robbed by a player who had mistaken soccer for volleyball.

During the press conference after the game, Luis Suarez, always controversial, said, "It was the best save of the World Cup. It pays to be expelled in this way.

"We suffered until the end but the hand of God now belongs to me," he concluded in reference to Diego Maradona's infamous handball of 1986.

**Fast Fact**

When South Korea faced Uruguay, Luis's grandmother asked him to give her a goal for Grandparent's Day. The Gunner scored twice, one for grandma and one for his grandfather Atasildo.

**The Sky Blue team celebrates Ghana's missed penalty.**

## Among the Four Best

It had not been the best way to win that game, but the Uruguayans showed the world that they were willing to do anything to move on. Their next opponent would be Holland, where Luis had starred for many years as a professional. The match was intense but Holland's team defeated the heroic Charruas, 3-2.

Germany and Uruguay clashed in the match that nobody wants to play: the third-place playoff on July 10, 2010. Luis was back on the field after the expulsion but it was not enough. Germany won a very good match against the Sky Blue by 3-2.

The Uruguayan National Team returned home with great pride in an honorable fourth place. They had achieved the best result by a team from Uruguay in the last 40 years.

# Light and Darkness

WHEN THE WORLD CUP TOURNAMENT ENDED, Luis Suarez went back to the Netherlands to begin the season with Ajax and try to add a new title to his trophy gallery. Before he could concentrate on soccer, however, what he describes as the "most beautiful experience of a lifetime" occurred.

Luis had married his girlfriend Sofia Balbi in March 2009. His civil wedding was in Amsterdam, while a religious ceremony was held in Montevideo. A year and a half later, in August 2010, Sophia gave birth to their first child, a daughter they named Delfina. As a messenger of good news, the heiress arrived in a superb time in her dad's life: Luis had just played a spectacular World Cup and had ended the season with more than 45 goals; he had also become a champion in Holland. As a good father, Suarez

promised to give his daughter everything she would need. The only thing he asked in return, jokingly, was that the baby not become a fan of Peñarol, Nacional's staunch rival.

## Bunny or Cannibal?

At the end of that summer of 2010, Luis and his followers themselves thought that he would next move to Spain, specifically to play for Barcelona. His transfer could not be made due to differences between the teams and Suarez

**Luis and Sofia hold their daughter Delfina during an Ajax match played while Luis was suspended from the team.**

would have to wait another year with Ajax. Immobility emotionally affected the Uruguayan, who along with his team fell into a rut of play. Supporters and players went into despair and Luis Suarez became the media punching bag.

It was in this context that the first of several controversies occurred. The stage was a league match between Ajax and hated rival PSV Eindhoven. The game was very heated. Both teams were kicking each other and things were going out of control. In the midst of a fight, Luis lost his temper, went to the Dutch player Otman Bakkal, and bit him in the neck. Although the referee did not see this, the cameras in the

Several soccer players, including Sebastian Abreu, Diego Lugano, Diego Perez, and Alvaro Gonzalez, attended the wedding of Luis and Sofia in Montevideo. Their story could be made into a movie. The couple met in 2002. At the ceremony, the couple's relatives surprised them by projecting a video with pictures of them when they were teenagers.

stadium captured the incident.

The images were seen around the world. How could a professional player, in his prime, do something like that? Worse, the referee let him continue playing. Days after the incident, Ajax passed a two-game suspension for Luis. However, the Eredivisie disciplinary commission suspended the striker for seven games.

The media, which dubbed him "the cannibal of Ajax" was relentless. Luis said he was hugely embarrassed and sorry for the bite. "I feel very bad about biting. The worst thing . . . is harming another person and I have apologized for what happened in Holland. It's something I regret, but it's in the past now."

It would not be the first nor the last headache that Luis's temperament would give his team. After the bite incident, many predicted the end of his career in the Netherlands. Luckily, his goals were powerful and there was no shortage of interest in other European clubs.

## Farewell to the Dutch

On January 28, 2011, an offer from England decided Suarez's future. The club Liverpool FC was willing to pay more than 23 million euros for the Gunner, an amount that Ajax could not refuse. The team captain's departure did not arrive at the best time, but his teammates made sure that Luis had the recognition he deserved.

The heartwarming farewell took place at the Amsterdam Arena stadium. After the

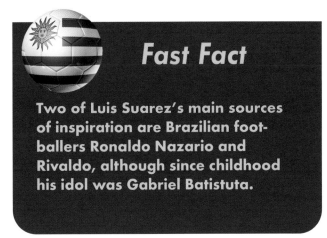

match, Luis said a few words and then fireworks filled the sky with multicolored light; thus ended a valuable four-year apprenticeship. Suarez had arrived during the 2007 season and remained with Ajax until 2011. In those four seasons, he scored 111 goals, a feat achieved by very few.

## Magical Mystery Tour

Suarez arrived to a declining Liverpool team that was placing high hopes in him. The pressure was great for the striker. At the time of recruitment, he was the most expensive player in the club's history. He had asked for the shirt with the number 7, a legendary number in that club because of the brilliant players who had carried it, such as Kenny Dalglish and Kevin Keegan.

His first game as a Red, on February 2, 2011, was a dream debut at home against Stoke City. With only a few minutes in the field, he scored his first goal in England and the first at Anfield Road to lead his team to victory by 2-0. It was the ideal start and it ignited the hopes of fans. Suarez however came at a difficult time for all: Liverpool was in the twelfth place in the

Liverpool manager Kenny Dalglish presents Luis and new signing Andy Carroll on February 3, 2011. When he was ten, Luis used to play as Liverpool on his PlayStation. Today his Facebook page has more than 1.5 million followers.

league and far from classifying tournaments in Europe. Luis would have only six months to turn the situation around.

The Gunman continued to have great performances and his goals helped Liverpool to climb into the league's sixth position. In his thirteen games with Liverpool, Luis scored four goals and five assists to finish the first season in England as one of the winter's best signings.

Meanwhile in Holland, Ajax finished as champion in the year of Suarez's departure. In a display of great courtesy, they invited Luis to the celebration. In his four seasons defending Ajax's shirt, Suarez had never been a champion, and since they had played with him half of the season, he was awarded a medal for what he had contributed in the first half of the season. Luis finished the 2010-2011 season with 16 goals, 12 were for Ajax, which put his two teams on the road to success.

## Copa America

After the club season, Uruguay and Luis Suarez had the opportunity to attend their next major competition, the 2011 Copa America. After its outstanding performance in the FIFA World Cup, the Sky Blue team was a serious candidate for the title. Luis felt that the best thing that could happen to them was to arrive as just another team and show their value in the field but the truth was that everyone had Uruguay as his favorite. Luis won critical acclaim in the semifinal. He scored twice against Peru and sent the Sky Blue team to the final, aiming at its fifteenth American title.

## At the Top of the World

The final match was riveting. Uruguay's national team began with an early goal in the 11th minute. That goal could not be someone else's: Luis received the ball inside the area and with a cut he left the Guarani defender confused. A left-footed shot froze the goalkeeper and the ball hit the goalpost before completing its journey into the net. The advantage of that first goal enabled the Sky Blue to become the crowned champion of the 2011 Copa America. Luis was recognized the best player of the tournament, over other stars like Lionel Messi and Diego Forlan himself. He was also the second-best scorer and the best man of his team.

**Luis receives the MVP award for the 2011 Copa América.**

Luis fights for the ball during a 2012
match between Liverpool and SK Rapid.

Chapter

5

# The Uruguayan Hope

LUIS SUAREZ BEGAN THE 2011-2012 SEASONS SCORING more goals for Liverpool, thus earning a secure place in the team. He helped the Reds beat Arsenal in London for the first time in over a decade. He scored against Everton in the classic game of Liverpool, and against Manchester United in the longstanding rivalry of English soccer.

To put the icing on the cake, on November 1 Luis was nominated for the FIFA Golden Ball award. However, controversy followed him. On December 7, 2011 he was accused of misconduct, so a file was opened to look into the case. Two days earlier, on December 5, Suarez had made an obscene gesture to the audience. The English Football Association (FA) penalized him, arguing that the lack of respect for the fan is a complete breakdown of the moral code of English football and it could not be ignored. Luis accepted his mistake and days later he took his sanction: a one-game suspension.

## More charges

On December 20 Luis received a new penalty for another offense, this time one that was more serious. It happened during a league match on October 15. The Gunman had offended Manchester United's Patrice Evra, calling him "negro" eight times. He was accused of racism. This time Luis was banned for eight matches and had to pay a fine of £40,000.

In a 115-page document the FA stated that Suarez had "damaged the image of English football around the world." According to the minutes, Luis had told Evra: "I don't speak to blacks" and responded "Because you're black" when asked why he had kicked the player. After hearing Luis's excuses, the striker was sanctioned and could not continue the season as he wanted. Overall, he had lost 16 games for suspension in the last two years, a high number for an elite soccer player. Luckily, Luis's talent and goal instinct outweighted his bad behavior—so far at least.

## The Bad Boy of Soccer

After the painful charge of having made racist comments—which much diverted the attention from what really mattered, his soccer ability—many said that Luis would leave English football. In his opinion, the FA was already after him and would look for any excuse to damage his career and, incidentally, his club. He was immediately linked with world-class teams like

Barcelona and Real Madrid, which is certainly indicative of his great talent.

His technical ability and energy make him one of the most lethal strikers in the world. With proper training and greater maturity, Suarez could become one of the best players on the planet. Luis, just turned 25, delights a packed Anfield stadium that cheers him enthusiastically every time he plays for Liverpool.

Always at the center of controversy, this "bad boy" of soccer makes enough tantrums and goals to remain on the front page of sports newspapers. He has also made time to do humanitarian work. He has supported the efforts of an organization called "Taking Conscience" in its fight against discrimination, and also the Richard Allen Foundation of South Africa. "I worry about social inequality," said the Uruguayan star who spent difficult times as a child. "And soccer has this huge potential to unite people, without distinction of color, religion, or social status."

## Hard Days

Because of his volatile temperament, Luis Suarez has almost left soccer twice. His bad behavior on the field is well-known. With incidents as biting another player, making obscene gestures to Fulham fans, or saving a goal with his hand, Luis is hardly a good example for younger players and he acknowledges this. "I want to learn to be calmer in the field," Luis has said. "I am still young and I've made mistakes, but only because I want to win."

This lack of discipline can be a threat to a brilliant career that is on the rise. On the other hand, Luis is one of the most effective strikers in Europe and therefore in the world. No wonder he has been targeted by other clubs like Arsenal, Chelsea, Milan, Juventus and Real Madrid.

As for his beloved Sky Blue, the Uruguayan team, he will certainly be summoned to the next World Cup in Brazil in 2014. He will then try to improve the fourth place that Uruguay won in South Africa. The playoffs have begun, and the Charruas are working toward earning their ticket to the next World Cup.

## The Gunner Strikes Again

In November 2011 the Gunner played what was perhaps his best game with the national team. In the qualifiers for Brazil 2014 he scored four times against Chile, all of them spectacular goals, and thus became the first player to achieve that feat since Romario. "I just found out," he said, "that no one had scored four goals in a playoff. I appreciate that a lot and I know that the fans were ecstatic."

After the bitter experiences in England, the threats from the European football authorities and the public relations disaster, Luis Alberto Suarez, that young man from Salto who had left Uruguay at 18, left the field cheered by a public that, in ecstasy, chanted his name. Washington Tabarez, the coach of the national team, did not hide his admiration. He acknowledged that Luis is at his peak.

"You feel a little like crying and butterflies in the stomach," he said after that game, where he could attest his people's support in difficult times. "As a child I was always a fan of the Uruguayan team and I suffered a lot. Today, when I heard everyone in the stadium chanting my name, I was very moved because I remembered tough times." In the end he refused to acknowledge that he is today one of the best players in the world. "I try to do my best, for my club and for the National team. I am just another player and I appreciate everyone's efforts."

Luis can be sure that everyone else appreciates his effort too.

**Fast Fact**

**Luis Suarez has a market value estimated at 35 million euros.**

# FURTHER READING

Bueno, José Antonio. *History of Futbol*. Spain: Editorial Edaf, 2010.

Figueredo, Alejandro. *I Was There*. Uruguay: Editorial Aguilar, 2010.

Groba, César. *The Lords of the Bow*. Uruguay: Groba Ediciones, 2003.

Lissardy, Ana Laura. *Go as We Will: One Team, One Country*. Uruguay: Editorial Aguilar, 2011.

Reyes, Andrés. *History of the Naational Team*. Uruguay: Editorial Aguilar, 2008.

Singer, Marcelo. *Closer to the Sky*. Uruguay: Editorial Zona, 2010.

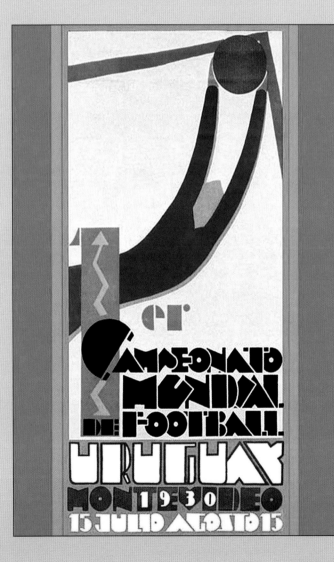

Poster for the 1930 World Cup tournament, which was held in Montevideo and won by La Celeste. Uruyguayans hope that young stars like Luis Suárez will one day win the cup.

# INTERNET RESOURCES

**www.luissuarez.co.uk**

Luis Suarez official site. Includes the Liverpool player's biography and interviews, photo gallery, press releases, videos and a brief description of Luis's social initiatives with NGOs. Available in English and Spanish. Managed by Media Base Sports, Luis Suarez Spain-based representatives.

**www.fifa.com**

Official website of the FIFA, the international governing body of football where you can find information about players, national team rankings, championships, awards granted by FIFA, and the latest news about soccer. Includes an extensive historical section and the ability to access the site in five languages, including English and Spanish.

**www.liverpoolfc.tv**

Official site of Liverpool soccer team. Includes player profiles, club history, schedules, results, and information about future matches. The online store offers official merchandise and tickets to team games.

**www.futbol.com.uy**

Portal for news, information, and commentary about Uruguayan soccer. Includes information on national teams, Uruguayan championship results, and videos of the best plays.

**http://en.wikipedia.org/wiki/Luis_Suárez**

Wikipedia entry about the Uruguayan player. Includes biography, personal life, club participation, and national team statistics, as well as useful external links to more material about Luis Suarez.

# INDEX

Abreu, Sebastian, 15, 22
Adiyiah, Dominic, 6
Ajax, 12–13, 20, 21–23, 24
Amsterdam, 13
Argentina, 7
Arsenal, 29

Bakkal, Otman, 23
Balbi, Sofia. *See* Suarez, Sofia Balbi (wife)
van Basten, Marco, 13
Batistuta, Gabriel, 7
Barcelona, 10, 11, 21, 28
Brazil, 29

Carroll, Andy, 24
Cavani, Edinson, 15, 17
Copa América, 24–25
Copa Libertadores, 8, 9

Dalglish, Kenny, 23, 24

El Salvador, 8
England, 23, 24, 27–28
Evra, Patrice, 27, 28

Feyenoord, 13
Figueroa, Elias, 11
Forlán, Diego, 6, 15, 16, 17, 25
France, 16

Germany, 19
Ghana, 5–6, 18, 19
Gonzalez, Alvaro, 22
Groningen, 11–12, 13

Holland, 11, 12, 13, 19, 22, 23

Keegan, Kevin, 23
KNVB Cup (Dutch Cup), 13

La Plata, 7
Liverpool FC, 23, 24, 26, 27–28
Liverpool Football Club of Montevideo, 11
Lugano, Diego, 7, 22

Manchester United, 27
Maradona, Diego, 18, 28
Messi, Lionel, 25
Mexico, 16, 17
Montevideo, 7, 9

National Football Club, 7–8, 9, 11

Partisan, 12
Peñarol, 21
Perdomo, Ricardo, 8
Pereira, Maxi, 15
Perez, Diego, 22
PSV Eindhoven, 23

Real Madrid, 28, 29
Rotterdam, 13
Romario, 29

Salto, 6–7, 29
Silva, Bruno, 11, 13
South Africa, 5, 6, 15, 16
South Korea, 17, 18
Spain, 10, 11, 21
Suarez, Delfina (daughter), 21, 22
Suarez, Luis
    and 2010 World Cup, 5–6, 15–19
    birth and childhood of, 6–8
    with national team, 4, 5–6, 12, 14, 15–19,
        24–25, 29
    professional career of, 7–8, 9, 11–13, 20,
        21–24, 26, 27–29
Suarez, Paolo (brother), 6, 7, 8
Suarez, Rodolfo (father), 6, 7
Suarez, Sandra (mother), 6
Suarez, Sofia Balbi (wife), 9–10, 11, 18, 21,
    22

Tabarez, Washington, 15, 16, 29

Urreta, 7

World Cup, 5, 6, 15–19, 29